The Army of God

Secrets of the chosen warriors

Thomas D. Burns Sr.

ISBN:9781797403656
ISBN-3:

ACKNOWLEDGMENTS
THIS IS FOR MY CHILDREN

The very reason that you are here on earth is to enjoy your will, and while doing so the inner you should continue to seek God until he comes or calls you to do some miraculous works in this lifetime. I truly hope that you have been through no rough times that he hasn't comforted and supported you in my absence just know that I would rather be with you. Although I am trying, I will probably never be able to fix every one of your problems, I will be here to go through them with you. I am writing these books because I am trying not to fail at getting you back and showing you my love as I always have. I will take the blame for allowing you to grow without me by doing so I have allowed you to live as God intended for you to live until he is ready for use to join unite and activated ourselves for his will to be done on earth as it is in heaven.

I TRULY LOVE EACH AND EVERY ONE OF YOU!

CONTENTS

DEDICATED TO

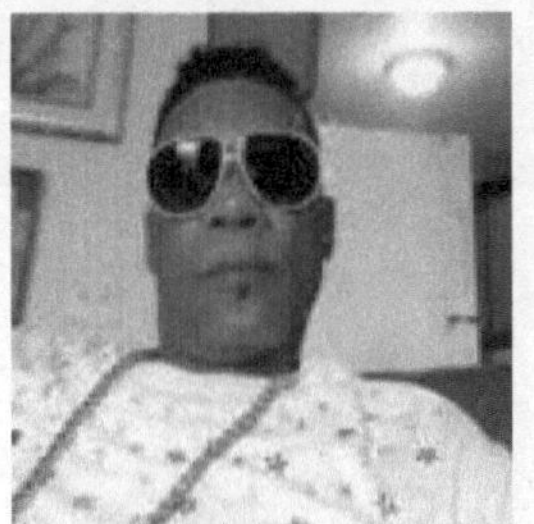

LEONARD K. WASHINGTON

Thanks for taking the time to read this and also other books of mine, and various others we truly appreciate you..

The Army Of God
The Secrets of the chosen warriors

By: Thomas Dennis Burns Sr.

CHAPTER 1.

INTRODUCTION

The mere thought of eternal life is perhaps the most doubted and controversial and or mysterious, of the ages, without a reasonable answer explaining its impossibility.

Without reading any one persons mind almost everyone has heard at least one person speaking on the topic of living forever and wanted to discover if it was indeed a realistic possibility for mankind to achieve in this lifetime to carry on for an eternity through hundreds maybe even thousands of years or even Light-years into evolution.

Here in this very literature is a secret message, hidden in the manuscript that will open your third abode and join your three existences with the elements that create life and regenerates the physical self with the inner self and the other remaining elements of nature, which we will get a lesson on later in the text.

When the words in the book of Genesis was proclaimed to have been discovered according to text one of the oldest scrolls found after the flood which had once been hidden in the family of Enoch's lineage since Enoch walked with God. During that time, there were Giants, of super human strength and they possessed powers that were of mystical essences and magical likeness.

CHAPTER 2. CAVE DWELLERS

My direct ability to tap into the spiritual me in a deep meditative like state of existence at any remote time, is where it all starts for me seeking answers, after three times dying for minutes and I mean hours on some occasions, it may seem like the opposite of a wanted experience. But I was just a child and of course I had no fear of death because the secret was still fresh in my mind and spirit that I have an eternal existence as well as a physical one.

The experience is not clear as it could be because I was so young, when I had great battles with a few different life threatening situations and injuries that ale me to this very day. Now there a many of practitioners of all sorts of crafts and works, that may occasionally misdiagnose their patients conditions, and somehow assumes that they are not quite as affected by any illness that they report and deny them the same remedies as others diagnosed with autism.

Whomever that judges or desires to be offended by something that I reveal to them about a coming or mysterious secret to the life we live and why we're here now after God was angry with man and the angels and caused the great flood that left no one besides Noah's family safe.

It will not be true to say that God killed every living thing that had evil in it, if in fact, there is a story of Noah's son Ham getting him drunk and performing some sexual acts with him leaving him naked.

Now keep in mind that this happened after they left from the ark and landed on the hill in a cave where Noah and his family settled. That would

mean that bad blood was yet still upon the earth and just like Cain and his entire bloodline upon bloodline was sent far away from others because of a curse and was not mentioned of his children or grandchildren just like we heard of Noah's children but never of his grandchildren looked at as mentally incapable.

The Lord Jesus Christ has been a mystery since the World began. Adam failed to become a god, so God became Man so Adam might just become a god. Islamic angels are said to have fallen after the creation of humans, but the Christian angels fell before the creation of the humans. It took Satan nine days to recover from his fall. When he rose from his fall he went to stalk Adam and Eve. They were new to the Garden Of Eden. "The mind is its own place, and in itself can make a Heaven of Hell, a Hell of Heaven" said John Milton for instance. In every think tank and soul pit there should be order and it takes a very conformed group of troopers to tend and mind such a facility considered to be a jail or a prison for the physical is mind of humanity.

CHAPTER 3 THE HOLY

THE
HOLY
BIBLE

KING JAMES VERSION

CHAPTER 4 WARRIORS

If you have never been to war then you fear the likes of it, Not a second of one's life needs to be set apart from the rest of the world. Warriors need services to assist them with the visions of all of the blood and guts they are faced with during missions and battles around the world the number of mental patients are rising by the dozens by the second and the total disabled veterans list grows at a rapid pace and the government just sends the whole world offset. The best way to describe a survivor of war, warrior. The elite play with us like checkers and chess pieces and we just let them move us across the world when we ourselves should be on the way to battle for our freedom that's the kind of warriors that we need in the world today. The new way of making arrangements for war is via scope. On many occasions we will see pictures of war and of many other disasters and think that we know what it's like to be in a war but some of us really have no idea what is going on in the world we are being prepared for what is ahead of us we know that Donald Trump is starting up the next world war as early as summer 2019 we may be at battle with several countries as well as inner cities raging against state and county officials and lawmakers battling with civilians over fraud and malice. This is truly looking like Hitler authored the book of revelations and they are pushing the envelope.

CHAPTER 5 GOD'S CHILDREN

Insert a coin into a slot machine today you have about a one in one million chance at winning on the first draw, but what if you knew that you were connected to everything in the world and even the slot machine can be programmed from the inside that does not likely assist you with winning on a slot machine at all. You may have more luck at contacting deities and entities much easier than trying telepathy on a machine. In fact the very topic of God's children is a wonderful read. Children of God are brave and fearless little babies and angels with magical powers and skills far more advanced than others.

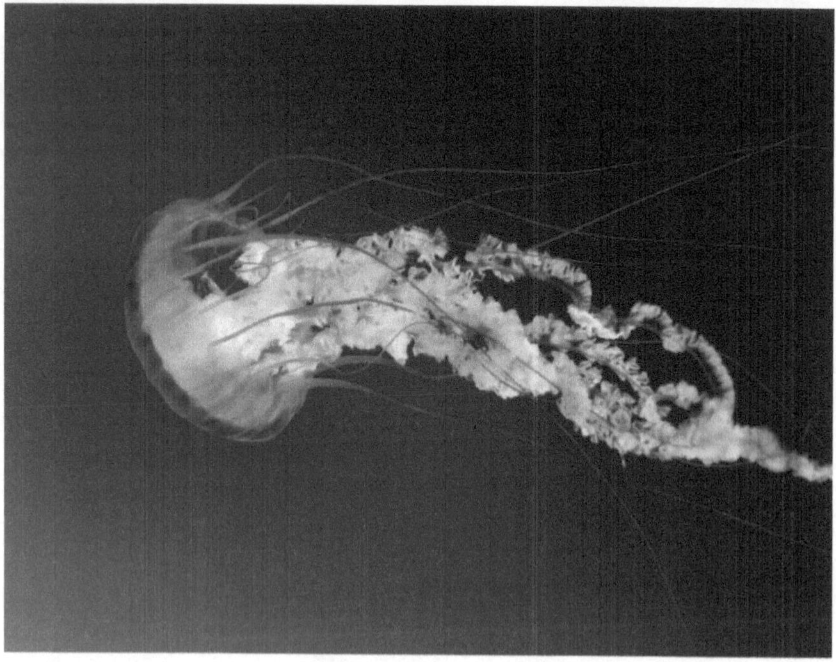

CHAPTER 6 FALLEN ANGELS

In full the book of Enoch was removed from the book of the Christian church this century we will be provided with a visual reading of the book's secrets and wanders blinding the very people that hid the truth from us all from the beginning of our ability to discover that America tries to dominate God and Gods worldwide. Taking a look into the near future we can see history replay itself over and over again and events of human depopulation schemes and ploys outright advancing this nation into war with heaven on absolute purpose just to see if God is proven to exist. Like it or not there are forces at work daily creating the next beast that will concur mankind in the end, horror is our everyday visual with pictures and images of disasters we need to reach a decision before we just let the wrong folks run the world while we were meant to rule over ourselves and our families. At home we hear witness of his wrath from our parents but we desire not to ever see his punishment only wish to receive his blessings if we are going to choose his way. Not a single person alive today has been able to see God clearly and visibly in person only when we leave the body can we see all this glory and marvel. We worship a master that brought us to a state of unconsciousness and has awaken us in another existence and we forgot who we were when we were born into these bodies we lost a bit of ourselves as the years went by we began to forget the father and we need to be growing closer and wiser toward and for the lord of hosts.

CHAPTER 7 WE ARE ALL GOD'S CHILDREN

In the beginning god created us and all things and then let us watch the entire thing and played all things to us as we were preparing to leave the spirit realm and enter into life sweet as we know it to be. Angels that came to adore humanity to the point of breeding with us and creating superior races of super human children and the Good guardians usually come to you in a time of need if it is the will of God they will intervene. Usually we think they on come to children. Maybe because later in life we can't see them. Could that be that we lose our innocence, is why we don't have the same ability to see angels as we grow older. Some of us even as a adult can see all kinds of Spirits. One day a little boy was starting out for class and he was struck by a car on the way across to get the train to his class, he was suddenly swept up and was set down as if someone picked him up and drifted him from worse damage.

CHAPTER 8 THE CHOSEN

In this chapter the sun and the moon, the stars and the elements of nature will be exposed for the reasons that we all must know to be at peace with life. First we all must close our eyes and visualize the blank solid blackness of all things.

Erasing the entire vision of what our eyes can see and activate the eyes of our minds and we will be able to picture the things that we want to see with The eyes of our minds and began to see what is to come by tricking ourselves with a false memory of the desired want, when done properly we can actually slip right into remembering the good things being delivered to us with the inner eyes, only then can we invite these desires into the dimension that we need them in.

According to reason, that is one way to attract the things that we need into our lives or we can just do the worse and take it from others and suffer the penalties as we know we will at the time we choose to do an act the laws of attraction prohibits wrongdoing.

Nothing about us has to be bad it is just a decision that we make to accept our laziness and lack of motivation and commit an act that we feel bad about later in life I have a personal knowledge of what is required of me and my children but I have no idea when or how I am supposed to get to the place because it is by spirit that we will be led to the exact place that we are supposed to be when certain things that our missions on earth leads us to the same places where we and others are used in the spirit by the inner spirit to provide the things that we need or others needed. We are all the spirit of god to the next spirit of god to the next spirit of god, which is why we are commanded to love thy neighbor as we love ourselves because we are all God's children the chosen and we were all with him when he spoke the words let there be light and when he said let us make man in our own image and likeness and we all were required to live in one of the bodies that we helped or perhaps we are the angels that watched as he created the bodies that our spirits were to inhabit like he built shells to put his spirit in and commanded us to multiply upon the face of the earth and to subdue it and cover it with bodies for the spirits of our seeds to grow and reproduce the eternal existence of human beings is through reproduction now we on earth are left to do his will on earth as he has and is doing in heaven at this very moment and we all are responsible for assisting god in keeping the human race alive and favorable to him. He has named us as gods after we ate from the tree in which he commanded us not to eat, and made for us clothes and gave us a land to rule over as the gods of a race of people that we created. We are all Adams and Eves, and are all given a chance to re-right the first wrongs we done to our heavenly father and after Jesus, showed us what we were capable of we still didn't ask him to teach us how we too can perform the same miracles that he so he didn't offer us the same because we didn't understand his way of thinking because he was different in his flesh as he was living on the inside and cared less for the outer man because he knew that the inner him was hidden from the world by the outer man and the acts outwardly of a person would reveal what lies deep within. Jesus knows and knew the same of the beginning as if he was a child in the new body that was given to a waiting spirit to reenter this world through a womb again and again. The way to look at reincarnation is to jump over to the left turn right quickly and you will see the body moves faster than thought and thought acts first in the process, why is it that your inner self controls all that you physically do in this life and the next as our spirit is the eternal matter within us all we have no idea why we are but we are here existing together and not trying to advance together to .

CHAPTER 9 GUARDIANS

In the continuum we are already eternal. We alone are saved by the sacrifice of Jesus if we believe that he died for the remission of our sins we will be able to live a more happy and free life knowing that we can do all things through Christ we acknowledge that we too have some ability to do more than what we are being taught on this earth to make comfort in our lives and in the lives of others around us. God loves us so much that the angels came to Adam and Eve and worshiped them as Gods because they were the us God was talking to when he said let us make man in our own image an likeness, as well as, "behold The Man Has Become As one of us, to know good and evil: and now, lest he put forth his hand, and take also of the tree of life, and live forever". Six years in a row man has the ability to allow himself to be free of religion and he denies his sacred covenant with his creator after discovering his true purpose to emulate God and all He has done. All of the atrocities that have happened in this world can make one wonder if God really with us. The Catastrophic events on earth such as Armageddon was one of the worst examples of human suffering. Those poor people prayed to God, but did he answer their prayers. What makes one have so much hate for another, just because of their religion? We are all part of the human race, what we believe in shouldn't become, the death of us.

CHAPTER 10 WHO ARE WE THEN

The very cause for knowledge of future events is ultimately because of the term (Watchers), The creator of all life in the universe is plural not singular, if viewed by most Hebrew scholars. (e.g.). "Elohim", a word that defines many.

The word Elohim is most commonly referenced to when speaking of human judges and false Gods or Tzeva'ot when namely it is discussing armies. "Let us make man", in our own image and likeness is a secret within itself.

If the angels that fell from heaven taught, mingled and procreated with humans the beginning was right when the angels left heaven to descend upon the daughters of man and saw that they were beautiful, they took for them wives and went into them and bore the children that God's spirit was so powerful in, that they were treated and worshiped as God's on the earth, enslaving the humans that did not as they commanded if not killed them all together.

David was an example of how the spirit of God can encourage even a small to be victorious at battle against a Giant superhuman being and win the battle. Saying that we are all a part of God's DNA actually if you think about it God is the spirit within each and every one of us which is why he will neither leave nor forsake you he is within us and we are within him and her is why we are created in our Gods image. Imagine if eve had children with Satan becoming the reason that they all were sent out of the garden of Eden, Cain definitely would be the child and can be proven by the acts that followed his brother Abel being born. Cain would be the source of Satan and God's spirit residing in the human DNA makeup. Keep in mind that Cain committed the very first murder and was exiled by God to a life of wandering in a distant land called Nod (Hebrew: Eretz -Nod), located "on the east of Eden" (qidmat- 'Eden), After he murdered Abel out of jealousy.

There is no time for focusing on the goals of the wicked yet there is still time to get ready for the war of heaven on earth. My mother saw an angle once. I don't know what she saw, but her face was nostalgic. For an instant I wondered what a angel may look like.

There are plenty of great minds of today that believes in God and his Angels. When I was about eight I was touched by "a angel". It was late, so it was bedtime. My mom got me ready for bed. Me and my sister shared a room, but she was at a friend's house.

I never liked that room. Trying to be a good kid I laid down. Mom left the door cracked, but it was still pretty dark. I heard voices coming from the other room. I so badly wanted to go play with my friends that had come over. Knowing my mom wouldn't let me, I stayed in bed. After a few minutes of wishing I was on the other side of the door, I felt something touch my foot.

At first, I thought it was the dog, but there is no way the dog could touch me like that. I sprang up to see where the dog was, except there was no dog. I would have seen the door open if it were. I didn't see it move.

Not sure what had happened I tried to go to sleep. That wasn't going to happen. My little heart was racing not sure what to do. As I got older that incident always made me wonder, what really happened that night.

All I can say about it is…I must have been touched by "a angel".

ANGEL

The world is in for a big surprise and will be shocked about the lies and myths of generations are about to be exposed and uncovered in the coming months of 2019. Many conspiracy theorists have provided their ideas and we have read as many as we could and still have not completely been able to provide ourselves with the totality of the knowledge of all things.

This is the first body of literature that equips it's readers with modern ways to deal with today's and future life events to come and how to prepare themselves for the activation of God's Warriors on earth during the latter days. You know who you are and he does too we all have the spirit of Satan, God and of the Goddess.

These three DNA make ups, have and will forever allow us to evolve and advance back into the beginning of all things if we meditate on heaven and god's purpose for each and every single one of us.

ABOUT THE AUTHOR

Thomas D. Burns Sr. is a native of Detroit, Michigan that is an American Writer and Author of Several Writings and Songs. His Materials can be found world round publicly. I invite you to discover his other works by searching for books and music by Thomas D. Burns Sr. online and in stores across the universe. For free. The Proceeds of this book is not by any means to be withheld from The Children of The Author.

DAWAN
MAKE IT ENOUGH
Dawan
Really Let Your Hair Down
gofundme
Global Radio Promotion
ONE LOVE

UNIVERSAL LIFE CHURCH MINISTRIES

Credentials of Ministry

THIS IS TO CERTIFY

Thomas Dennis Burns

That The Bearer Hereof Has Been Ordained

On this day, the 25th of December, in the year 2018
and is officially recognized as a member of the Universal Life Church
and has all rights and privileges to perform all duties of the ministry.

CHAPLAIN, BR. MARTIN

KAQOE
INTERNATIONAL
WORSHIP
CENTER
FOUNDER
PROPHET THOMAS D. BURNS SR.
(419) 901- 6308
godslaw18@outlook.com
http://kaqoeworshipcenter.simplesite.com

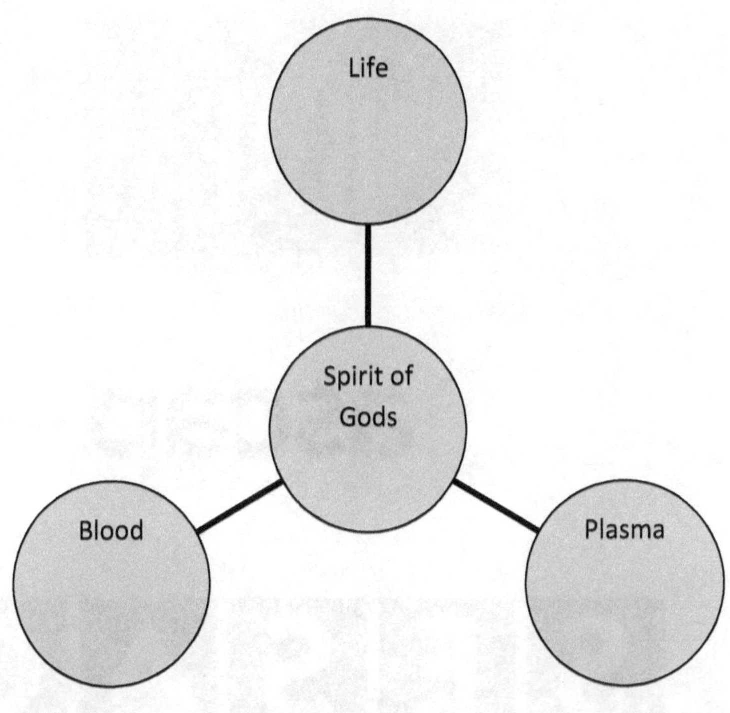
Life
Spirit of Gods
Blood
Plasma

BMI

ascap

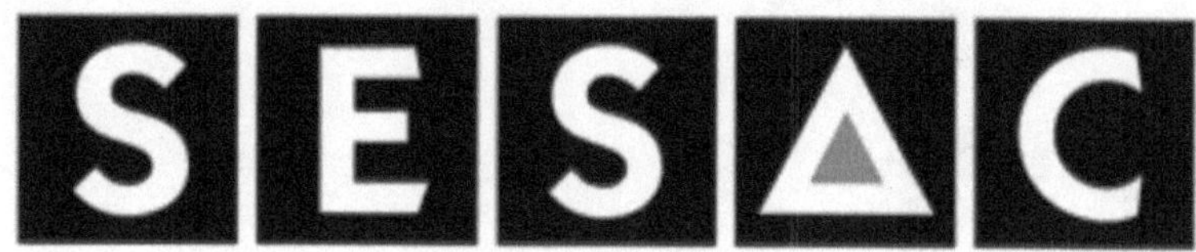
SESAC

Lord Rama

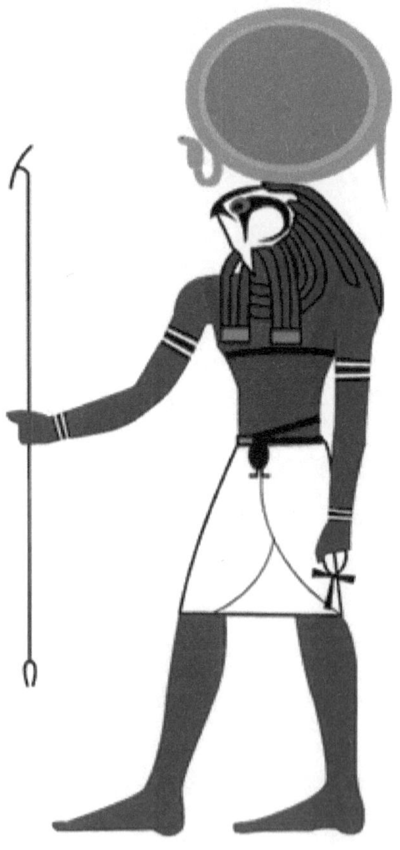

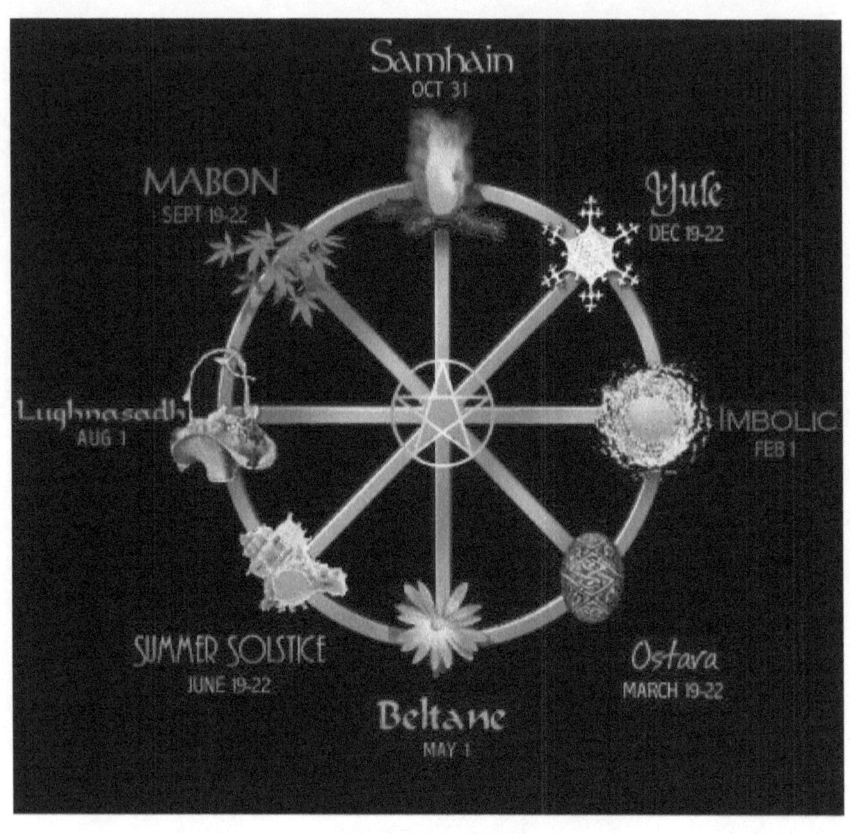
Samhain
OCT 31
Yule
DEC 19-22
IMBOLIC
FEB 1
Ostara
MARCH 19-22
Beltane
MAY 1
SUMMER SOLSTICE
JUNE 19-22
Lughnasadh
AUG 1
MABON
SEPT 19-22

Dark King
Gold
Old King
Myrrh
Frankincense
Young King

FOR WHERE TWO OR THREE
ARE GATHERED TOGETHER IN MY NAME,
I AM THERE IN THE MIDST OF THEM.

Jeremiah
29:11
For I know the plans I have for you, declares the Lord, plans to prosper you and not to harm you, plans to give you hope and a future.

WOUNDED WARRIOR
PROJECT

www.ingramcontent.com/pod-product-compliance
Lightning Source LLC
Chambersburg PA
CBHW031420250726
48656CB00002B/748

* 9 7 8 1 7 9 7 4 0 3 6 5 6 *